1, 2, 3,
It's Easy for Me!

Tracy Kompelien

Consulting Editors, Diane Craig, M.A./Reading Specialist
and Susan Kosel, M.A. Education

ABDO
Publishing Company

Published by ABDO Publishing Company, 4940 Viking Drive, Edina, Minnesota 55435.

Printed in the United States.

Credits
Edited by: Pam Price
Curriculum Coordinator: Nancy Tuminelly
Cover and Interior Design and Production: Mighty Media
Photo Credits: AbleStock, ShutterStock, Wewerka Photography

Library of Congress Cataloging-in-Publication Data

Kompelien, Tracy, 1975-
    1, 2, 3, it's easy for me! / Tracy Kompelien
    p. cm. -- (Math made fun)
    ISBN 10 1-59928-505-3 (hardcover)
    ISBN 10 1-59928-506-1 (paperback)

    ISBN 13 978-1-59928-505-4 (hardcover)
    ISBN 13 978-1-59928-506-1 (paperback)
    1. Counting--Juvenile literature. I. Title. II. Title: One, two, three, it's easy for me! III. Series.

QA113.K658 2007
513.2'11--dc22

                           2006012847

SandCastle Level: Transitional

SandCastle™ books are created by a professional team of educators, reading specialists, and content developers around five essential components—phonemic awareness, phonics, vocabulary, text comprehension, and fluency—to assist young readers as they develop reading skills and strategies and increase their general knowledge. All books are written, reviewed, and leveled for guided reading, early reading intervention, and Accelerated Reader® programs for use in shared, guided, and independent reading and writing activities to support a balanced approach to literacy instruction. The SandCastle™ series has four levels that correspond to early literacy development. The levels help teachers and parents select appropriate books for young readers.

Emerging Readers
(no flags)

Beginning Readers
(1 flag)

Transitional Readers
(2 flags)

Fluent Readers
(3 flags)

These levels are meant only as a guide. All levels are subject to change.

To count is

to add numbers together
to find a total, or sum.

Words used
when counting:
even
how many
number
odd
quantity

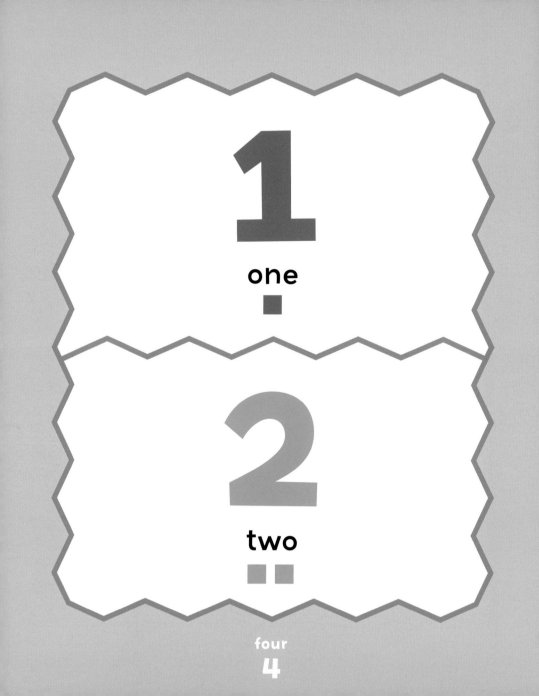

1

one

2

two

3

three

4

four

5

five

6

six

7

seven

☐☐ ☐☐ ☐☐ ☐

8

eight

■■ ■■ ■■ ■■

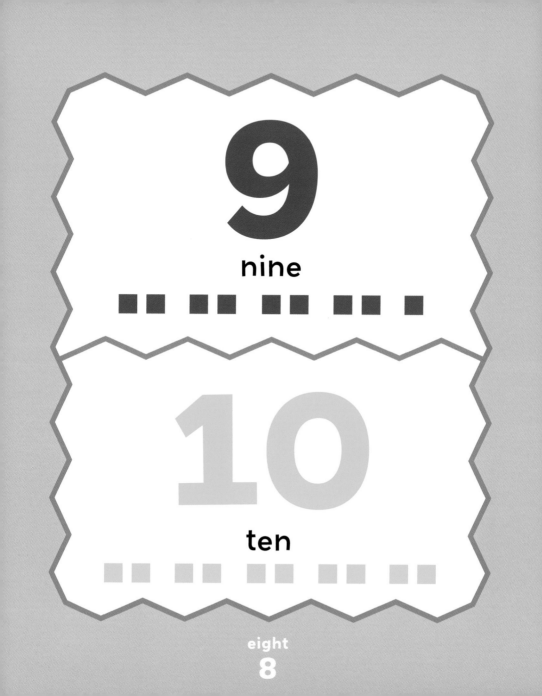

9

nine

10

ten

0

zero

I know that this is zero because there aren't any blocks to count. Zero means the quantity of nothing, or none.

1, 2, 3, It's Easy for Me!

As Carl counts **1**, he says, "This is fun!"

One is an odd number. I know that this is an odd number because it cannot be grouped in twos!

twelve
12

Carl counts **1**, 2, 3, 4.

"I want to count some more!"

Four is an even number. I know that this is an even number because it can be grouped in twos! Four makes two pairs.

fourteen
14

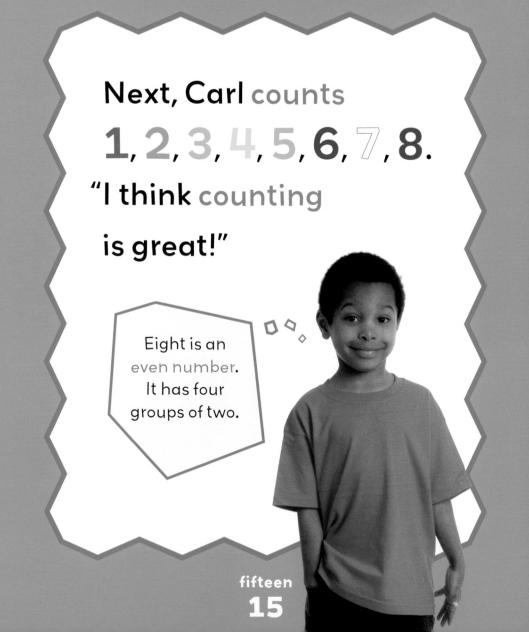

Next, Carl counts

1, 2, 3, 4, 5, 6, 7, 8.

"I think counting

is great!"

Eight is an
even number.
It has four
groups of two.

Counting Every Day!

Coty counts **2**

 on his feet.

eighteen
18

Coty counts 5 fingers

on each .

twenty

20

When Coty plays soccer,

he brings 1  .

Coty counts the  on his shirt. How many are on your shirt?

Glossary

count – to add numbers together to find a total or sum.

even – a number that can be grouped in twos with nothing left over.

number – a word or symbol that shows how many or how much.

odd – a number that cannot be grouped in twos. There is always 1 left when odd numbers are grouped in twos.

quantity – a countable amount or number.